# Ken Moser

Published in 2013 by 10Publishing, a division of 10ofthose.com

9D Centurion Court, Farington, Leyland PR25 3UQ, England.

Email: info@10ofthose.com Website: www.10ofthose.com

ISBN 978-1-909611-49-8



Printed in the UK

Luke: Carry Your Cross

# Contents



leader's notes available through

**www.effectiveyouthministry.com**

## Luke: Carry Your Cross

# Introduction

### Welcome Carry Your Cross!

Some people think of Jesus as a teacher who tells us "to be kind" or "try your best to be good." In reality, Jesus demands that we follow him with our all of our heart, soul, mind and strength. He calls us to leave the crowd, walk the narrow road of faith and sacrifice everything for him.

Following Jesus means that we must die to ourselves so that we may truly live. Get ready: these studies are not for the faint of heart nor those who don't want to take Jesus seriously. While carrying the cross of Jesus and walking the narrow road can be tough, in the end, it brings true life.

Enjoy this radical teaching from the giver of life!

**Ken Moser**

Luke: Carry Your Cross

# Love Your Enemies

## Luke 6:27-36

"But to you who are listening I say: Love your enemies, do good to those who hate you, bless those who curse you, pray for those who mistreat you." Luke 6:27-28

let's get started

## let's get started

1 When I see someone I really don't like, I ...
(place a ✔ in the appropriate box)

☐ Do evil things to them in my mind ☐ Get aggressive and taunt them
☐ Walk the other way ☐ Call my friends together for support
☐ Me? I love everyone! ☐ Other? ______________________

2 Have you ever had an enemy? Tell us about it.

going deeper

## going deeper

**Let's get the facts straight.** Read Luke 6:27-36.

+ Is there anything that immediately impacts you when you read or hear this?

**Turning the other cheek (vv. 27-31)**

+ List all the ways we are to respond to our enemies (or when bad things are done to us).

v. 27 ______________ v. 28 ______________

v. 28 ______________ v. 29 ______________

v. 29 ______________ v. 30 ______________

v. 30 ______________ v. 31 ______________

Now place a number from 1 -10 next to each one, rating how hard it is to do. (1= a piece of cake 10= impossible)

+ Why is it so hard to "turn the other cheek" when wrong is done to you?

+ Have you ever not retaliated when you could have?

**Being different from everyone else (vv. 32-36)**

+ Jesus describes unbelievers three ways here (vv. 32-34). What three things do they do?

1. ______________ 2. ______________ 3. ______________

+ How are we to be different from them? List all the ways given here (see v. 35)

______________________________

______________________________

+ What are the promises given to those who "love their enemies"? (v. 35)

+ According to v. 36, why are we to be merciful?

+ When you read this, did anyone in particular come to mind? In other words, is there someone with whom you need to put this teaching into practice? Do you think you can do it? Why/why not?

**Jesus says it again. Read Matthew 5:43-48.**

+ What are the extraordinary things that Jesus tells us to do in this part of the Bible?

+ Why are we to love our enemies? (vv. 45 & 48)

- What would happen if you put this teaching into practice…

| In your school? | At home? | On the sporting field? |
| --- | --- | --- |
| | | |

| When you are out socially (like at the shopping mall)? |
| --- |
| |

**The Apostle Paul agrees.** **Read Romans 12:14-21.**

- How do you feel when you read this? (Circle and explain your answer.)

Oh no, not again

This is just too tough

Ok, ok… I get the point

I can do it

I'll try to do it

I have no enemies I am a friend to all

something else? ______________________________

- How can you overcome any struggles in living out these commands?

- Is it possible for you to not take revenge when someone harms you? (v. 19)

**Helping each other**

- How can we help each other to live out this difficult teaching?

- What do we need to change?

- What would you say to someone in this group who confesses, "I just don't think I can love some people I know?"

## let's pray

- Pray that we will love those who harm us.
- Pray that we will love those we don't like.
- Pray for the strength (and grace) to implement this radical teaching from Jesus.

## stay tuned

Next week, we explore the cost of following Jesus!

# For your eyes only:
# The week ahead

# For your eyes only: The Week ahead

## 1. Personal Bible Reading

This series of Bible reading will be in the Gospel of Matthew. You may find many stories that are familiar to you (Matthew has many similarities to Luke). This week, we will read chapters 1-5. In these chapters, you will find the story of Jesus' birth and early ministry.

### My weekly Bible reading plan!

In the Gospel of Matthew, I read (place a ✔ when you have read it.)

Chapter 1 ☐ Chapter 2 ☐ Chapter 3 ☐ Chapter 4 ☐ Chapter 5 ☐

## 2. Memory Verse

Can you learn the memory verse below (Luke 6:27-28)? Give it a try this week.

**"But to you who are listening I say: Love your enemies, do good to those who hate you, bless those who curse you, pray for those who mistreat you."** Luke 6:27-28

Pray for all the people in your life whom you find difficult to get along with. Pray that you will be patient and gracious with them. Pray that God will change your heart, so that you can love them and show kindness to them.

Things that I can thank God for: ______

Things that I need to pray for: ______

**Hot tips for being kind towards someone you don't get along with**

1. **Pray. Pray. Pray.** Keep asking God to give you strength to love them and to be good to them.
2. **Work on holding your tongue.** Jesus tells us to "turn the other cheek" (Luke 6:29). This means that we must be willing to take insults and persecution without retaliating. Try to learn to not respond to an insult or taunt.
3. **Remember your memory verse.** When you see someone that you don't like, send up a quick prayer and think about your memory verse from this study ("Love your enemies....").
4. **Try and spend time with those you don't like.** It may be difficult, but quite often, you will find common ground and may even learn to be friends.
5. **Remember that God set the example for us.** He demonstrated his own love by sending Jesus to die for us while we were his enemies! (Romans 5:8)

# Following Jesus Costs Everything

## Luke 9:23-27

**Then he said to them all: "If anyone would come after me, he must deny himself and take up his cross daily and follow me" Luke 9:23**

let's get started

## let's get started

**1** How do you feel when you are told that you must "put God first in your life"? (place a ✔ beside your answer)

- ◯ I don't mind ◯ I plug my ears and make a loud noise
- ◯ I fall on the ground and throw a tantrum ◯ I've never heard this before
- ◯ Sometimes I try to do it, sometimes I don't
- ◯ I don't know what it means to do this ◯ Other? ______________

**2** Have you ever had to give up something in order to follow Jesus? If so, what was it?

going deeper

## going deeper

**The cost of following Jesus, Part I: Carrying your cross**

**Read Luke 9:23-27.**

+ When you read this, what are your first impressions?

In your own words, what do you think these phrases mean? Can you give practical examples of each one?

» Deny himself and take up his cross daily

» Whoever wants to save his life will lose it, but whoever loses his life for me will save it.

» What good is it for a man to gain the whole world, and yet lose or forfeit his very self?

» If anyone is ashamed of me and my words, the Son of Man will be ashamed of him

+ Why is it tough to put Jesus first all the time? How can we do a better job?

+ Why do you think Jesus wants us to "lose our life"? Does this mean he wants us literally to die?

+ Have you ever met someone who has stopped following Jesus in order to "gain the whole world"? What happened?

+ Have you ever been ashamed of Jesus? What was the situation? What would you have done differently if you could?

FYI

**Carrying your cross = death!** If you lived in the time of Jesus, you knew exactly what it meant to "carry your cross". If you saw someone with a cross, you knew that they were on their way to die. This was meant to be the ultimate in final humiliation. It told all who were watching that you were to be punished and there was no way out—you were going to your death. When Jesus was going to die, he had to carry his cross so that we might have life (See John 19:17). When Jesus tells us to carry our cross, he is calling us to die to ourselves, in order to find life in him.

**The cost of following Jesus, Part II: Following Jesus will cost a lot**

**Read Luke 14:25-35.**

+ When you read these words from Jesus, does anything immediately impact you?

**vv. 25-27**

+ What is the point he is making to "the crowds"?

+ Do you think he wants you to treat your family with "hatred"? What is he saying?

**vv. 28-35**

+ What is the point these two stories are making?

+ Look at v. 33 again. How does this verse sum up what Jesus is saying in the previous stories?

+ What does it mean to "give up everything"? Does this mean we are to have no possessions?

+ What does it mean to be "salty"?

+ Have you ever known someone to "lose their saltiness" when it came to following Jesus? What was the cause?

+ What can you do to make sure this doesn't happen to you?

## getting active

**Helping each other**

+ How can we help each other live out the radical teaching in these two Bible passages?

+ Is there anything that we need to change, in light of today's study?

## let's pray

- Pray that we will not let anything get in the way of following Jesus.
- Pray for wisdom and strength to know how to deal with things that may try to take us away from the faith.

## stay tuned

Next week, we see the sacrifices we must make to follow Jesus!

# For your eyes only:
# The week ahead

# For your eyes only:
# The Week ahead

## 1. Personal Bible Reading

This week, read Matthew chapters 6-10. This section contains the "Sermon on the Mount" (chapters 5-7). This is some of the most challenging (and famous) teaching in the whole New Testament.

### My weekly Bible reading plan!

In the Gospel of Matthew I read (place a ✔ when you have read it.)

Chapter 6 ☐ Chapter 7 ☐ Chapter 8 ☐ Chapter 9 ☐ Chapter 10 ☐

**Get rid of everything that keeps you from Jesus: Hebrews 12:1-3**

Read this passage from the Bible. (The "great cloud of witnesses" (v. 1) are those people who were listed in chapter 11. They are a "who's who" of great Bible men and women.)

- Why is it so important to stay focused on Jesus as you try to live as a Christian?

- Is there anything that you need to get rid of that is hindering or tangling you?

## 2. Memory Verse

Can you learn the memory verse below (Luke 9:23)? Give it a try this week.

**Then he said to them all: "If anyone would come after me, he must deny himself and take up his cross daily and follow me."**

**Luke 9:23**

## 3. Prayer

Pray for help to constantly deny yourself and follow Jesus. Pray that you won't devote yourself to things that will keep you from being a strong Christian. Ask God for strength to say "no" to anything that could block your relationship with him.

Things that I can thank God for: ______________________________

______________________________

Things that I need to pray for: ______________________________

______________________________

**Helpful hints to "deny yourself, carry your cross and follow Jesus"**

1. **Many of your friends won't understand this concept.** Most people these days are taught to look after themselves first. The idea of living for God instead of yourself is unusual.
2. **Be prepared to be treated the same way Jesus was treated.** Our Lord was mocked and ultimately killed by those around him. People may also insult and laugh at you.
3. **Putting Jesus first will mean sacrifice.** You may have less money, friends, time and possessions. Remember what Jesus said, "What good is it for a person to gain the whole world yet lose their soul?" (Luke 9:25). The important thing is to keep your soul strong by following Jesus.
4. **Begin today.** Many Christians put off sacrificing until "later." (An example of this is waiting to give money to the church until you have a "real job.") Learn to do things now that require sacrifice. This includes putting sports and study second to youth group and church. Another example is to spend time with someone who really needs a friend even when you have "so much to do."
5. **Less is more.** Your life will not be judged by the number of possessions you own or the amount of study you have done. Your life is about getting to know God and serving him. Keep this as your focus. This will free you up from the traps and tangles that many people fall into.
6. **It is easier to do it with a group of other Christians.** Keep meeting with your small group and keep going to youth group and church. Stay connected with a group of people who want to follow Jesus and serve him.

Luke: Carry Your Cross

# Following Jesus = Sacrifice (But It's Worth It)

## Luke 9:57-62

"What good is it for a man to gain the whole world, and yet lose or forfeit his very self?" Luke 9:25

## let's get started

1 **Share** Have you ever gone hungry, spent a miserable night out, or thought that you might not have a nice place to sleep?

(For example, your family got lost looking for a motel, or you were trying to find a campground late at night)?

Tell the group about it!

2 Would you still follow Jesus if you...

(Place a ✔ for yes or a X for no next to each statement.)

___ Had to be poor the rest of your life?

___ Had to die for him?

___ Would never get a girlfriend/boyfriend (or marry) because of your faith?

___ Would have to sell your favorite possession and give the money to the poor?

**Following Jesus may not be easy.** **Read Luke 9:57-62.**

- Is there anything that immediately impacts you from this story?

- What point is Jesus making…

  to the 1st man? (v. 58) ______

  to the 2nd man? (v. 60) ______

  to the 3rd man? (v. 62) ______

- What is the overall message Jesus is giving to these three men?

- Why do you think Jesus is saying it would be difficult for these men to follow him?

- Have you ever met people who wanted to follow Jesus but dropped out when they found out what it takes?

- How confident are you that you can follow Jesus even when times get tough? (Circle your answer.)

I'll never give up!

I think I can do it

I'll give it my best shot

It may be a struggle, but I'll try

Not sure

Something else? ______

What's the question again?

**A case study in following Jesus: The rich young ruler.**
**Read Luke 18:18-30.**

- Do you think the ruler was genuine in his questioning of Jesus (or was he just trying to justify himself)?

- Why was Jesus not satisfied with all the good things the man had done?

- What was the young man's real spiritual problem?

- Do you think Jesus wants us all to make the same sacrifice? Why/why not?

- What was the promise Jesus gave him if he would do what Jesus asked? (v. 22)

- Why is it hard for rich people to get to heaven? Does this story mean that no one with money will get in? (See v. 27)

- What does this story ultimately teach us about following Jesus?

**The Apostle Paul's experience of following Jesus.**
**Read 2 Corinthians 11:24-29**
- How do you feel after reading this list?
- Which of these things would be the worst experience for you?
- Would you be willing to go through the same things Paul went through?

(If you want more on Paul's experiences, read 1 Corinthians 4:11-13.)

## getting active

**Helping each other**
- How can we prepare ourselves for any sacrifices that may come because we follow Jesus?

- Is there anything in our lives that blocks us from following him?

- How can we help each other to put into practice what we have learned today?

## let's pray.
- Pray that we will be willing to make sacrifices and go through hardships because we follow Jesus.
- Pray that we will always stay strong as Christians and stay focused on following Jesus.
- Pray that we will be willing to get rid of anything that keeps us from following Jesus.

## stay tuned
Next week, we will look at what Jesus says about worry and stress!

# For your eyes only:
# The week ahead

# For your eyes only: The Week ahead

1. Personal Bible Reading

This week, read chapters 11-15 from the Gospel of Matthew. If you haven't kept up, try to read as much as you can this week.

**My weekly Bible reading plan!**

In the Gospel of Matthew, I read... (place a ✔ when you have read it.)

Chapter 11 ☐ Chapter 12 ☐ Chapter 13 ☐ Chapter 14 ☐ Chapter 15 ☐

**God will help you make it!**

The Bible tells us that God doesn't leave us on our own—he helps us to follow him. Read each passage, answer the questions below and reflect on the help God gives us as we try to follow Jesus.

John 10:27-30 Romans 8:31-39 1 Corinthians 10:13
Philippians 1:3-6 (See also Isaiah 41:10 & 43:1-7)

- What promises are given to us in this passage?

- What does this passage tell us about God?

## 2. Memory Verse

Try to learn the memory verse below (Luke 9:25).

**"What good is it for a man to gain the whole world, and yet lose or forfeit his very self?" Luke 9:25**

## 3. Prayer

Pray for strength to follow Jesus no matter what happens. Pray for wisdom to know when things are keeping you from following Jesus.

Things that I can thank God for: ______________________________

______________________________

______________________________

Things that I need to pray for: ______________________________

______________________________

______________________________

**FYI Suffering can be good for you (believe it or not)!**

We have seen in this week's study that following Jesus can be tough. It is important to know that the Bible tells us that a lot of great things can come through our suffering for Jesus.

**Read Romans 5:1-5 (especially vv. 3-5).**

+ Reflect on the three things that result from suffering for Jesus. Do you know what each of these means?

**Read James 1:2-4**

+ Why should we accept trials, according to James?

+ Have you ever gone through a hard time because of your faith? What was the outcome?

The Bible has a lot more to say about suffering for Jesus. Read these verses from the Bible, and reflect on how can you learn to accept suffering and not lose heart.

Matthew 5:11-12
1 Peter 1:6-9 & 4:12-19
2 Corinthians 4:7-12 & 6:3-10 & 12:7-10
Revelation 2:8-11

Luke: Carry Your Cross

# Don't Worry

## Luke 12:22-34

"Therefore I tell you, do not worry about your life, what you will eat; or about your body, what you will wear. Life is more than food, and the body more than clothes." Luke 12:22-23

let's get started

### let's get started

**1** What worries me the most is/are: (Place a ✔ in as many boxes as you want)

- ☐ school
- ☐ my friends
- ☐ my brothers/sisters
- ☐ having/not having a boy/girlfriend
- ☐ troubles in this world
- ☐ the way I look
- ☐ the future
- ☐ my parents
- ☐ money
- ☐ homework
- ☐ me, I've got no worries
- ☐ Something else ______________________

**2** My stress level right now is....

1 ------------ 20 ---------- 40 -------------- 60 ------------ 80 ----------- 100

cool as a cucumber — so-so — stressed to the limit!

**Let's get the facts straight:** **Read Luke 12:22-34.**

+ What two illustrations does Jesus use to tell us not to worry? (vv. 24-28)

1. ____________________

2. ____________________

+ Why are we not to worry about physical necessities such as food and drink? (vv. 29-31)

+ What does Jesus really want us to be concerned about? (v. 31)

+ What does this look like in everyday life?

+ What is the radical response Jesus wants us to make instead of worrying? (vv. 32-34)

+ Why?

+ Is he telling us that food and clothing will magically appear if we trust in him?

**A case study in dealing with anxiety: Mary and Martha.**

**Read Luke 10:38-42.** (Mary & Martha were good friends of Jesus. Their brother, Lazarus, was the guy Jesus raised from the dead in John 11.)

+ Why was Martha so upset at Mary? (v. 40)

+ What did Jesus say to her? (vv. 41-42)

+ What should Martha have done instead?

+ Have you ever had so many things to do that you neglected your relationship with Jesus (and his people)? What should you have done instead?

- What makes you like Martha ("worried and upset about many things") instead of like Mary (who "has chosen what is better")?

**"When you are in a fix, turn to Philippians 4:6!"**
Read this verse (and v. 7 as well) and answer these questions:

- What is the solution to anxiety; according to this verse?
- Why do you think this is so?
- Why should thanksgiving accompany our prayers?
- What does the Apostle Paul promise will come to us, if we bring our stresses to God? (v. 7) Why do you think he promises this?
- Have you ever been stressed out, prayed to God and felt much calmer afterward? If so, share it with the group.

## getting active

**Helping each other**

- How can we help each other to put into practice what we have learned today?
- Is there anything that we need to do differently?
- What must we do when we start to get stressed or anxious?

## let's pray

- Spend some time sharing what is causing anxiety for you. Pray as a group for each of these.
- Pray that we will seek God's kingdom.
- Pray that we will not be too busy to spend time with Jesus.
- Pray that when we are anxious we will turn to the Lord in prayer.

## stay tuned

Next week, we will see the need to repent and follow Jesus.

For your eyes only:

# The week ahead

# For your eyes only: The Week ahead

## 1. Personal Bible Reading

This week read Matthew, chapters 16-20. (If you need to, try to spend some time this week catching up.)

**My weekly Bible reading plan!**

In the Gospel of Matthew, I read... (place a ✔ when you have read it.)

Chapter 16 ☐ Chapter 17 ☐ Chapter 18 ☐ Chapter 19 ☐ Chapter 20 ☐

## 2. Memory Verse

Can you learn the memory verse below (Luke 12:22-23)? Give it a try this week.

> **"Therefore I tell you, do not worry about your life, what you will eat; or about your body, what you will wear. Life is more than food, and the body more than clothes."** Luke 12:22-23

## 3. Prayer

Pray each day for your stress level and anything that causes you anxiety. Ask the Lord to help you to turn to him whenever you feel anxious. Pray that you will not become so busy that you will forget about spending time with him. Are there things that you are anxious about right now? If there are, pray for each of them right now.

Things that I can thank God for: ______________________________

______________________________

Things that I need to pray for: ______________________________

______________________________

**Hot tips for dealing with worry, anxiety & stress**

1. **Keep meditating on the Bible passages in the study above.** God's word is designed to help and strengthen us. Memorize Philippians 4:6, and read Luke 12:22-34 often.
2. **Pray, pray, pray!** Keep taking your stresses to God. He wants to help.
3. **Are you doing too much in your week?** Go through your schedule, and see if there are things you can drop out in order to give you more time to focus on the important things. Many of us fill our time doing way too many things. In this day of stress and anxiety, we need to trim away those things that aren't necessary.
4. **Learn to manage your time.** Spending too much time online, playing video games, texting friends or watching TV can increase your stress level. This is because you are using valuable time doing things that could wait. Take a good look at your behavior, and figure out if there are things you need to drop out.
5. **Remember the story of Mary & Martha (Luke 10:38-42).** This story reminds us to be committed to those things that are truly important. Stay committed to reading your Bible, praying, and meeting with other Christians regularly. If there are things in your life that are making it impossible for you to do this, it is time to cut some things out of your schedule.
6. **Take a day off.** Take a week off! It is important to take a day off each week (it is, after all, a commandment—see Exodus 20:8-11!). You will be amazed at what this can do for your stress level. When you have a break in your school calendar, take a few days off and just relax and unwind. This is the time for you to hit the games, chat online and text to your heart's content. You may find it difficult at first (to take time off), but once you get in the habit, you will learn to love it.
7. **Know yourself.** We all need different ways to refresh. For some of us, it means being with people. Others need time alone. Some need to read a novel; others need to take a walk outdoors. Figure out what things you need to do to help you stay sane.
8. **Stay healthy.** Get plenty of sleep. Eat healthily and exercise regularly. You'll be surprised at what this can do to keep your stress levels down.
9. **There are times when you will need to talk with someone about the stress you are feeling.** This could be a professional counselor, your parents, your Bible study leader, youth minister or the minister of your church. Don't be ashamed or embarrassed to go to someone for wisdom and help.
   Many of us have needed to do that.

Luke: Carry Your Cross

# Repent and Enter Through the Narrow Door

## Luke 13:22-30

"Make every effort to enter through the narrow door, because many, I tell you, will try to enter and will not be able to." Luke 13:24

let's get started

### let's get started

1. If someone said to you, "It is hard to get to heaven," how would you respond? (Circle your answer)

No problem, I'll do what it takes

Umm, don't know

Doesn't everyone go to heaven?

Tell me something I don't know

I think I can, I think I can

What was the question again?

something else? ______________________

2. Do you think most people believe it is easy to get to heaven?

**Jesus tells us to "enter through the narrow door"**
**Read Luke 13:22-30.**

- Have you ever wondered how many people are going to be in heaven?

- How does Jesus answer the question that is asked him (v. 24)? What do you think this means?

- What is the meaning of the story in vv. 25-30?

- What is the ultimate fate of those who didn't really know the owner of the house?

- What does this story tell us about getting to heaven?

It is very common for people to say, "There are many ways to heaven," or, "It is really easy to get to heaven."

- How would you respond to this, in light of this Bible teaching?

**Let's look at this from a different angle: Read Matthew 7:13-14.**
Does anything impact you right away when you read this?
Jesus tells us there are two options. Give a description of each one.

| The wide gate, broad road | The narrow gate |
|---|---|
| | |

- Describe what this Bible passage means for us in everyday life.

- What do we need to do to make sure we stay on the narrow road?

**1 Corinthians 9:24-27: Run the race in order to win!**

- What does this passage tell us about following Jesus?

- What will it mean for you to:

  *"run in such a way as to get the prize"*

  *"not run aimlessly"*

  *"beat your body and make it a slave"*

  *"not be disqualified for the prize"*

## getting active

**Helping each other**

- Is there anything in your life that could keep you from "entering through the narrow door"?

- When is it easier to cruise along with the crowd, rather than to walk the narrow road?

- How can we help each other to put into practice what we have learned today?

- What changes do you need to make in your life to ensure you walk the narrow road?

## let's pray

- Pray that we will always strive to follow Jesus, no matter the cost.
- Pray that we will never grow weary in following Jesus.
- Pray for anyone we know who is struggling with his/her faith.
- Pray that we will get rid of anything that keeps us from being strong Christians.

## stay tuned

Next week, we will learn about building our lives on solid rock rather than sand!

# For your eyes only:
# The week ahead

## For your eyes only:
# The Week ahead

### 1. Personal Bible Reading

Hopefully you have kept up with in Matthew (If not, try to catch up.). This week, read chapters 21-24.

**My Weekly Bible Reading Plan!**

In the Gospel of Matthew, I read... (place a ✔ when you have read it.)

Chapter 21 ☐ Chapter 22 ☐ Chapter 23 ☐ Chapter 24 ☐

**Read Hebrews chapters 10-12:**
**Keep following Jesus, stay focused, don't give up.**

The book of Hebrews was written to a group of Christians who were being persecuted for their faith. Because of this, they were tempted to give up following Jesus. Read Hebrews 10:32-12:29 (if you don't have time to read it all, read 10:32-39). **Answer these questions:**

- How does your situation compare to theirs?
- Why must we never give up?
- What must we do in order to stay strong in our faith, according to this Bible passage?

Spend some time reflecting and praying about your relationship with Jesus. Are you in danger of growing weary as you follow Jesus? Is there anything you need to do to strengthen yourself?

Can you learn the memory verse below (Luke 13:24)?

**"Make every effort to enter through the narrow door, because many, I tell you, will try to enter and will not be able to."** Luke 13:24

## 3. Prayer

Pray that you will follow Jesus in all that you do. Pray for strength to follow him, even when it is difficult.

Things that I can thank God for: ______________________

______________________

______________________

______________________

Things that I need to pray for: ______________________

______________________

______________________

______________________

### For your reflection

In light of today's study, you may need to spend some time reflecting on your relationship with Jesus. **Thoughtfully consider these questions:**

- Are you in danger of growing weary as you follow Jesus?
- Have you repented of your sins? (For more on this, read Psalms 32 & 51 and 1 John 1:8-2:2.)
- Do you feel that you have "entered the narrow door"? In other words, have you turned to Jesus and put your trust in him only?
- Is there anything keeping you from turning to Jesus and trusting in him?
- Is there anything you need to change, in light of today's study?

Spend time praying that God's Spirit will help you to continue to grow in your faith. If you think it would be helpful, you may want to contact your small group leader and spend some time chatting through these questions.

# Don't just listen to Jesus, do what He says. The Wise and Foolish Builders, Luke 6:46-49

"But the one who hears my words and does not put them into practice is like a man who built a house on the ground without a foundation. The moment the torrent struck that house, it collapsed and its destruction was complete." Luke 6:49

let's get started

## let's get started

1. Have you ever listened to someone in authority and then *not done* what they told you to do?
(A school teacher? Parent? Babysitter? Boss at work? Someone else?)

2. If someone was to give you a score on "doing what Jesus says," what score would you get? (Place a mark somewhere between 0 and 100)

0 -------------- 20 ----------- 40 ------------- 60 -------------- 80 ----------- 100

rotten ok bullseye—I'm the best!

3. How is disobeying Jesus different from disobeying someone like a school teacher or your boss?

**Do what Jesus says:** **Read Luke 6:46-49.**

- Why do you think Jesus is so forceful in what he says (v. 46)?

- What is the clear point of the story in verses 47-49?

- What did the first builder do that was right?

- What did the second builder do that was wrong?

- Can you give practical examples of being a "good builder" (doing what Jesus says) and a "bad builder" (not doing what Jesus says)?

| "good builder" | "bad builder" |
|---|---|
| | |

- What kind of "floods" (i.e. hard times and difficulties) will force you to need a secure house?

**Listen to Jesus:** **Read Luke 8:19-21.**

- Is Jesus being mean towards his family?

- What does Jesus want from those who claim to follow him? (v. 21)

- Have you ever met someone who claims to follow Jesus but doesn't appear to obey what he says? What should you say to people like that?

**But wait, there's more!**

If there is time, choose one of these passages and answer the questions below:

**Psalm 119:9-16** **Matthew 7:21-23** **James 1:22-25**

- What does this tell us about listening to the word of God and doing what it says?

- What does this tell us to do/not do?

- How does this Bible passage relate to the story Jesus told about building on the rock?

## getting active

**Helping each other**

- How can we help each other to listen to Jesus and do what he says?

- Give some practical examples of "hearing God's word and putting it into practice" (Luke 8:21).

## let's pray

- Pray that we will do what God's word tell us to—even when it is hard.
- Pray for anyone we know who claims to follow Jesus but struggles with obeying him.
- Thank God that he has given us his word as a firm foundation to build our lives on.

## stay tuned

Next week, we will have another great Bible study!

# For your eyes only:
# The week ahead

## For your eyes only:

# The Week ahead

### 1. Personal Bible Reading

This week, finish this great Gospel. Read the last three chapters (26-28).

**My weekly Bible reading plan!**

In the Gospel of Matthew, I read... (place a ✔ when you have read it!)

Chapter 26 ☐ Chapter 27 ☐ Chapter 28 ☐

### 2. Memory Verse

Can you learn the memory verse below (Luke 6:49)? Give it a try this week.

**"But the one who hears my words and does not put them into practice is like a man who built a house on the ground without a foundation. The moment the torrent struck that house, it collapsed and its destruction was complete."** Luke 6:49

### 3. Prayer

Pray this week that you will live in a way that reflects the teaching of Jesus. Pray that you will do what he says, even when it is difficult or unpopular. Pray that your friends will "build their houses on the rock".

Things that I can thank God for: ______

______

______

______

Things that I need to pray for: ______

______

______

______

**Building on the rock vs. building sand castles: hot tips for doing what Jesus says every day.**

Living for Jesus and building on the rock of his words can be difficult. Here are some ideas to help you to build on solid rock.

1. **To build on the rock of Jesus' words, you need to know what he says.** Get to know his words by reading the Bible as often as you can. Read, reflect on it and try to memorize it.
2. **To build on the rock effectively, you need God's help!** Pray that God will help you to remember what you read in the Bible. Pray that he will give you the strength to do it, as well. Start each day by asking God to help you do what Jesus says.
3. **Building on the rock is a lot easier if you have friends and support.** Make sure you have people around you who encourage you in following Jesus and discourage you from building on the sand.
4. **When you fail and stop doing what Jesus wants you to, remember that God can forgive you and wants you to start again.** Get off the sand, go back to Jesus and start again.
5. **Try your best to become a person who helps others to build on the rock.** When you go to youth group, encourage others in the group to follow Jesus as well. Does your school have a Christian group? If it does, go to it and help the other students to build on the words of Jesus.

# thank you

Thanks to Belinda Hopper and Kathy Tyers for their proofreading editing. Thanks to Julie Moser for her editing. Thanks also to Sarah Smith for her work on the layout and graphics.

## Other recommended resources for your youth ministry:

### Small group Bible studies

Starting Out
By Ken Moser

Foundations For Christian Living
By Ken Moser

Luke: Who is Jesus?
By Ken Moser

Luke: Jesus' Parables
By Ken Moser

Death And Resurrection Of Jesus
By Julie Moser

Work Rest Play
By Ken Moser

Young Men
By Ken Moser

Young Women
By Julie Moser

Big Issues For Today's Youth
By Ken Moser

Studies 2 Go
By Julie Moser

More Studies 2 Go
By Julie Moser

### Resources for leaders

Programs 2 Go
By Ken Moser

Changing the World through Effective Youth Ministry
By Ken Moser

Creative Christian Ideas for Youth Groups
By Ken Moser

Youth Evangelism: Reaching Young People in a Way that Honours God
By Ken Moser